Letters from Slovakia is an interesting look into the society and culture of the Slovak Republic. David James describes life in Slovakia through a collection of letters that were first published on the Slovakia - Heart of Europe website, between the years 2002 and 2003. It includes the letters “Journey from Hell”, “Easter Traditions”, “World Champions” and the infamous “Christmas Shopping”.

Below are just some of the comments that visitors to the Slovakia - Heart of Europe site have made about David James' Letters from Slovakia:

"The Letter from Slovakia feature is GREAT! When are they going to be made into a book?"

"This travel journalist is very amusing..."

" ... and the Letters are extremely well written."

"Ďakujem for David James` letters. Especially the journal about making Kaputsa."

"I had to write and say how funny I found the Christmas Special Letter from Slovakia...."

"I really enjoyed your Letter from Slovakia this month. That was hilarious about the chickens..."

Second Edition

First Printing, 2012

ISBN-13: 978-1470190231

ISBN-10: 1470190230

Printed in the United States of America

Visit the website at www.heartofeurope.co.uk

Letters From Slovakia

David James

Heart of Europe Publications

Dedicated to the memory of
Mamúlik (1953-2009),
loving mother-in-law and friend,
and
Veronika Husáková (1978-2009),
our most wonderful Czech friend.
Both so brave to the end.

Letters From Slovakia

Preface

The second edition of Letters From Slovakia has been printed as part of the ten year anniversary of the Slovakia Heart of Europe website. These letters were first sent out to subscribers of the site's newsletter in 2002 and 2003, before being compiled into the first edition of this book, back in December 2003.

Letters from Slovakia is a humorous look at my personal experiences of this beautiful little country in the heart of Europe, from my first encounter with Slovakia in the summer of 1997, up until the close of my second year of actually living in the country, towards the end of 2003.

There is no doubt that Slovakia has changed a lot in the decade since these letters were first written, both for the better and for the worse, but many of the themes in the book still hold true today.

I hope that Letters from Slovakia will provide you with a glimpse of what life was like, for an Englishman at least, in this relatively young nation; some years on from the Velvet Revolution and the Velvet Divorce, but still prior to the country joining NATO and the European Union.

First Encounter

It was during a sunny morning in the summer of 1997, whilst trawling through a list of embassies in London, that I first came across Slovakia. I had just started a job selling a web-based tourism product and having exhausted all of the National Tourist boards, I was now working my way through a list of embassies, attempting to set up sales meetings.

Up until that day, I had only ever heard about Slovakia in the context of Czechoslovakia, the country in Eastern Europe that was hard to pronounce and almost impossible to spell. Of course I had heard of the Czech Republic, in fact I had called the Czech Embassy the day before trying to arrange a meeting. However, in my ignorance, I had thought that Czechoslovakia had just decided to change its name to the Czech Republic following the fall of Communism, or perhaps to make it easier on children around the world taking their geography exams. I had no idea at this point that Czechoslovakia had actually been made up from two unique nations that had peacefully gone their separate ways four years earlier.

My first reaction on discovering this new country was to feel quite pleased. Not because Slovakia had finally got its independence after a thousand years of waiting, but because the Czech Embassy had not agreed to a sales meeting, and so this was like a second bite at the cherry.

About two months later, I found myself walking down Kensington Palace Road on my way to the Slovak Embassy, and in my hand was a ticket for the Ambassadorial Champagne Reception, to celebrate Slovak Day.

You see, not only had I managed to get a sales meeting that morning when I phoned up the embassy, but when I went there a week later I ended up having a two hour conversation about Slovakia with the counselor, discussing such subjects as the Gabčikovo Dam and whether or not the country was ever likely to join the European Union. They didn't buy the product, but then I was never meant to be a salesman and I changed jobs quite soon after.

What happened at the Slovak Day reception will be the subject of a future "Letter from Slovakia", but needless to say I had a great time. And the invitations did not end there. I continued to receive more letters for over a year, inviting me to art exhibitions, poetry recitals, craft fairs, etc., which were all taking place at the embassy.

And it was thanks to the Slovak Embassy, that when I met my Slovak wife-to-be for the first time at a party the following March, I was able to present her with the perfect chat up line.

'Do you fancy going to a classical concert at the Slovak Embassy, on Saturday?'

An Invitation To The Embassy

"Champagne Sir?" said the waiter.

"Yes please," I replied, finishing off the glass I was holding and taking a new one from the tray.

I turned back round to the group of people I was with, and joined in the toast that someone had just proposed.

"Na Zdravie!" I said.

Well actually that's not exactly true. I probably said "Cheers!" or "Your health!" or even "Bottoms up!" But I definitely didn't say "Na Zdravie!"

You see, at the time I couldn't speak a word of Slovak. To be perfectly honest I hadn't realized that such a language existed, I probably thought our hosts were speaking Czech. Yet, despite my ignorance, there I was drinking champagne, eating caviar, and mixing with dignitaries, diplomats, ambassadors and MPs at a Champagne Reception inside the Slovak Embassy, in London.

* * *

A couple of weeks earlier, when I received the signed invitation from the Slovak Ambassador, it had come as a bit of a surprise. I had met with a counselor from the embassy a few months before, to discuss an online tourist service that helped promote countries in the UK. Although, the counselor was not very interested in the product, he was very hospitable and we ended up spending a further hour or so discussing politics, economics, tourism and culture.

It was then that I first learnt a little about the history and culture of Slovakia, and heard about the Gabčikovo Dam, the Tatra Mountains and the Velvet Divorce for the first time. As I went to leave, the counselor presented me with a tourism pack about Slovakia, which included a colorful, illustrated book and a CD-ROM with many photos of the country. I remember leaving the embassy thinking how charming and generous the people there had been. But even so, I was still very surprised when I received my invitation in the post.

So there I was, a fortnight later dressed in my best suit and with the invitation in my inside pocket, walking through Kensington Palace Gardens, on my way to the Slovak Embassy. I had been to a number of meetings with counselors from different countries over the few weeks prior to that day, so I was quite used to walking down the avenue of embassies that runs parallel to Kensington Palace. However, on that day the journey from the underground station had been a little different.

It was only days after Diana, the Princess of Wales and the newly crowned Queen of Hearts, had tragically died in a car crash, in Paris. The whole of Kensington Palace Gardens had become a shrine to her, with mourners laying wreaths and sympathy cards everywhere. I had been able to smell the flowers as I had left the underground, but it still did not prepare me for the scene I witnessed once I reached the palace gardens. It was like a sea of flowers. I don't think I had ever seen so many flowers. I too stood with the other mourners for a time, before finally continuing my journey to the embassy.

As I walked down the avenue of embassies and consulates, I recognized a few of the beautiful buildings as ones where I'd had meetings before. I passed the Royal Nepalese Embassy, the Russian Embassy, and many more. On and on I continued, until at last I reached the final two buildings on the street, which were in stark contrast to the others I had just passed. The first, a drab, gray affair, which looked like an old office block from the sixties, was in fact the Czech Embassy. Next to it, housed in an even more ordinary looking block, was my destination - the Embassy of the Slovak Republic.

Despite my longer than planned detour to Kensington Palace, I had still made it on time for the Champagne Reception. I fished out the invitation, from my inside pocket, and joined the queue. Once in the queue, it suddenly struck me what exactly was I doing there? I didn't know anyone, except for the counselor and he might not even be there, I didn't know anything about Slovakia and it was the first time in my life that I had been to something like this before. I suddenly felt quite nervous. I quickly made a plan - once inside, head for the champagne!

The queue continued right through to the reception hall, where people were introduced one by one to the ambassador and his wife. Having said hello to his Excellency, I got myself a glass of champagne and a plateful of nibbles, and went and looked for somewhere to stand. I spied an elderly, Asian gentleman, standing on his own and looking as uncomfortable as I felt, so I went and joined him.

I began to talk with the old man and discovered that he was actually from Vietnam. His English wasn't very good, and he seemed quite nervous, so he did not say that much but he did occasionally nod as I made comments about the weather and other equally uninteresting topics. I was just about to leave and get another glass of champagne, when we were suddenly joined by a group of people, one of whom said:

"Let me introduce you all to the Vietnamese Ambassador!"

I had been making small talk with an ambassador. Cool. I went and got another glass of champagne.

After a few more glasses of the bubbly stuff, I was beginning to feel more like networking, so I began to tag myself on to different groups of people. I ended up having an interesting conversation about Margaret Thatcher with a Conservative MP's wife, I spoke to a Minister from the island of Tonga, and also continued my conversation about Slovakia and the European Union with the counselor I had met earlier that month. However, my most interesting encounter came near the end of the soiree, just as I was thinking of making a move.

On the far side of the room there was a small exhibition, presenting a number of sculptures by a Slovak artist. There was also an interesting, full color book on display with a history of the sculptor's work. It was the last of many that had been given out over the course of the evening. The artist was Arthur Fleischmann, who had recently died aged 94, in 1990, and I learned that he was in fact one of the most important sculptors of the twentieth century. I read that amongst many other famous pieces, he had been commissioned to do a sculpture of Queen Elizabeth II and also of Pope John Paul II.

As I was reading about Fleischmann, a middle-aged woman and a young man in his early twenties approached me. The lady, who appeared to be in her fifties, began to speak to me.

"I know it's awfully rude of me, but do you mind if I have that book you are reading," she said. "It's just that I had promised it to this young gentleman."

"No problem," I said, handing her the book.

She proceeded to write a message in the front of the book and then signed it. I noticed that she had signed it Joy Fleischmann.

By now I'd had enough glasses of champagne to ask this lady who she was. I reckoned that she could either be Fleischmann's daughter or granddaughter. I decided to err on the side of caution.

"Are you Arthur Fleischmann's granddaughter?" I asked.

"No, actually I was his wife," she replied. And then added, when she saw my surprise. "I was quite young when I married him."

I continued to talk to Joy for awhile, and sensing that I was interested in her late husband's work, she promised to send me a signed copy of his book. A week later, my signed copy duly arrived in the post. To my surprise there was also a separate letter from the Slovak Embassy - an invitation to a classical concert.

I could get used to this, I thought.

The Journey From Hell

My first visit to Slovakia was in 1998, to spend Christmas and New Year with my wife-to-be's family. Having recently purchased our first house, and so watching our pennies somewhat, we made the trek half way across Europe by coach instead of by plane. We left Dover on the morning of the 22nd December, finally arriving in Brno, Czech Republic, at midday on the 23rd December. The journey was pretty much as you would expect a 30-hour coach journey to be. Awful.

Between us we had about seven items of hand luggage (one of which belonged to me), which we squeezed into the luggage rack above our heads, in the space reserved for our legs, and anywhere else we could find. One of the bags (the Christmas presents bag), which just couldn't fit anywhere else, took up half of my wife's seat. This basically meant that we had to endure a 30-hour journey sharing one and a half seat's worth of space and with no legroom whatsoever. Worse still, all of the videos, shown continuously throughout the night, were in Czech.

So even though I found myself in the seemingly envious position of being the only male onboard (with the exception of Vladimir and Boris, the coach drivers) cooped up with 40 stunningly attractive Czech and Slovak au pairs, all aged between 18 and 23, for over 30 hours - the journey was still pretty awful. As bad as it was, nothing in the world could have prepared us for the second leg of our journey, the five and a half hour trip from Brno to Ružomberok, in Slovakia.

Whilst queuing at Brno bus station (for two and a half hours) I hadn't really envisaged any problems in securing a seat on the 3:00pm coach to Ružomberok, seeing as we were third in the queue. I was wrong. When the bus arrived, on time I hasten to add, it was exactly that a single decker bus (as opposed to a coach) and was full; completely, totally and utterly full to the brim. For some unknown reason the bus driver opened the doors when he arrived at the stop, though not to let anyone off and surely not to let anyone on. I boldly pushed my way to the front and enquired of the driver when the next bus to Ružomberok would be.

What happened next was quite remarkable. On hearing of our plight of having to get to Slovakia before Christmas the driver got up from his seat and began to load our two suitcases and eight items of hand luggage (my wife had bought some more presents in Brno) into the front of the bus. We ourselves got on, stood between our luggage, and before we knew it, we were on our way to Slovakia.

At the time, as we left Brno coach station, I remember feeling quite guilty and also rather sorry for the two people we had queue jumped (I am British after all) to get on this the last bus to Ružomberok before Christmas. That guilt lasted all of ten minutes. In the UK, or in the States of course, it just wouldn't have happened. Safety laws just wouldn't have allowed it. There we were, on a bus with as many people standing as sitting, and that wasn't accounting for our luggage.

It wasn't long into the journey, perhaps 20 minutes or so, when my legs began to ache. Standing fixed to the spot, boxed in and unable even to adjust my stance, I soon realized that I could be stuck like this for over five hours - there was just no way I'd be able to last that long. Two suitcases, two food bags and a Christmas present holdall further up the bus stood my wife, seemingly non-plussed by our situation. Well I suppose at that point we had been standing for less than half an hour, and anyway it appeared that she had fashioned more space for herself between the bags and was able to vary her standing position from time to time.

During the next four and a half hours, of one of the worst travel experiences of my life, the bus must have stopped half a dozen times. To begin with I had logically seen this as my best chance of securing a seat. Yes, I had thought to myself, 20 people get off at Trenčin, and so 20 standing people are seated. So there I stood (obviously) and counted the seconds until we arrived at the first stop. Unfortunately, as it turned out only two people got off at Trenčin, only one of whom was up at my end of the bus and too far away for me to grab her seat. Instead, a middle-aged bearded fellow, three mini-rucksacks, a Christmas present bag and a handbag further up from my wife, grabbed the seat and barely before the poor old lady had vacated it. I could hear him let out a contented sigh as he lowered himself into his seat, like a king in his throne. I may have imagined it, but I'm quite sure I saw him smile at me, a smug sort of smile, which said 'I've joined the ranks of the seated classes, you standing person you!'

Deflated at the thought of standing until the next stop at Považská Bystrica, I now found myself faced with another problem. The old lady, who wished to get off the bus, was now busy trying to squeeze past my wife, almost tripping over one of the mini-backpacks as she did so. The next, and more difficult, part of this improvised assault course would involve the old lady getting past two huge Samsonite suitcases and me. In short, this was just not going to happen. The only possible solution was that I, the two suitcases, a Christmas present bag and two food bags, would have to get off the bus to let the old lady off. That done, I would have to load them all back on again, hopefully before the driver drove off.

This process took about five minutes, although it did seem to take a lot longer under the glare of a bus full of Slovaks, who seemed to watch my every move. As the old lady finally got off the bus she took my hand and thanked me and then smiled a toothless grin. This made me feel rather good, and I too smiled as I arranged the hand luggage back on the aisle of the bus, in a slightly different combination so as to create as much space for myself as possible. Then I went back for the suitcases. A man, seated at the front of thc bus must have felt sorry for me, as he got up from his seat and helped me lift the two Samsonites that I had been struggling with. While he was up helping me, I half toyed with the idea of stealing his seat, but quickly dismissed this wicked thought from my mind, and then felt extremely guilty after such a show of kindness.

The bus stopped a further three times before I was finally able to get a seat (incidentally my wife was seated after the second stop at Považská Bystrica). Two of those times I repeated my removal man act for the entertainment of the entire bus, aided once more by the kind hearted Slovak, who was called Ján. Each time I thanked Ján for his help, he nodded his head and said 'Okay, okay!' as if to reassure me that it was no trouble at all. I liked Ján. In fact, I decided there and then that I would like Slovakia - and those first impressions have been proved right ever since.

Since that day, I have used Slovak public transport on numerous occasions in my journeying throughout the country. On the whole, the bus and train services are very good, far better than in the United Kingdom, and at a fair price too. In fact, that first journey was the only bad experience I have ever had in Slovakia, and you have to remember that had we been in England we wouldn't have been able to get on the bus in the first place and may have spent Christmas, on our own, in some cheap Brno hotel.

The trip that my wife and I took from Banská Štiavnica to the beautiful little town of Kremnica last week, is a more typical example of a bus journey in Slovakia. It was a 30-mile trip, to the backdrop of stunning mountains, through the picturesque countryside where the unfortunately named "Hell" beer comes from. Ironically, that bus journey from Hell was an altogether more pleasant experience!

The Heart Of Europe

"Can we go now please?" asked my wife, as she took yet another picture of me pointing at the monument and grinning inanely.

"One more photo, please," I replied. "Make sure you get the actual words to prove we were here."

We were at the center of Europe, not far from a Franciscan Monastery, and just outside the little village of Kremnické Bane. A simple plinth, with the words "Stred Európy", marked the spot. We had made our way up a steep, windy road from Kremnica that morning, and found our way to the heart of Europe, more by luck than by judgement.

Now we could say that we had stood at the middle of a continent, and we had taken the photos to prove it. And now... well... well that was it.

There wasn't anything else to do here. There were no souvenir stands selling postcards from 'the center of Europe', Heart of Europe shaped fridge magnets, or books providing the proof that this really was the correct longitude and latitude. No 'Median Café' or 'Midpoint Restaurant' to serve you "Center of Europe Specialities". There was not even the usual old man, with a suspect looking uniform, charging you 10Sk to park your car by the side of the road.

You see, the Center of Europe is not commercial in the slightest, and when you think how some European countries might have milked it for all it was worth, it was actually quite pleasing that it was such a simple affair.

However, there are only so many photos that you can take of a plinth with the words "Stred Európy" inscribed on it. So literally 10 minutes after arriving, we left Kremnické Bane and the Center of Europe behind, and made our way back down the winding road to Kremnica.

* * *

Kremnica is without doubt one of my favorite places in Slovakia. There is a wonderful, relaxing atmosphere to the town, which is in perfect harmony with the surrounding Kremnica hills. It is the ideal environment to take a lazy, Sunday afternoon stroll and not have a care in the world, except perhaps whether the pub in the distance sells draught beer or not. Bliss.

However, Kremnica is in no way boring. Quite the opposite is true. For a relatively small town, with a population of no more than 7,000, there is a lot to see and do here, including two interesting museums, a gallery and of course the beautiful Kremnica castle, which majestically overlooks the town, from up amongst the hills.

And lets not forget the attraction that puts Kremnica on the map - its world famous mint. No, it's not a giant-sized, plastic Polo Mint in the town square, but rather a mint of the coin making variety, which is actually one of the oldest in the world, and one that is still producing Slovakia's coins today. It seemed quite natural then that we should change up some of our money here.

"Right, shall we get our traveler's checks changed up, and then plan our afternoon over lunch?" I suggested to my wife, as we parked the car in Kremnica's parking lot.

"It's okay, I'll go for the money," said my wife. "You can start reading the brochures and look after the bags."

I knew that this was actually so that she didn't have to put up with my moaning while we waited half an hour for our traveler's checks to be changed up. I was a little disappointed though, because watching 5 people consulting each other and various manuals for 30 minutes over a $50 check is quite fascinating. However, I didn't object, and she left me in a café terrace with our two backpacks, which were weighed down with the books, leaflets and brochures that we had picked up from the tourist information office that morning.

I picked out a leaflet entitled the 'The Town Castle of Kremnica', and began reading. I had barely begun to learn how 'the Charnel House is the oldest surviving building of the castle', when I felt a presence hovering over me, so I looked up. It was a waitress; I had forgotten I was in a café's terrace, so it took me by surprise. It suddenly dawned on me that I would have to use my Slovak, alone and without the usual five minutes preparation.

"Erm..." I said. To make matters worse she was young and extremely attractive. "Err..." The waitress smiled, obviously amused at my discomfort. "Erm..." Out of instinct I suddenly blurted out, "Prosim si Chilli Burger a jedno pivo, čapovane."

"Veľké?"

"Ano, prosím."

The waitress smiled again, and walked back into the café to place my order.

It was the first thing that had come into my head, I didn't even know if they had Chilli Burgers on the menu. Reading it quickly now, I saw that they did actually have them, as well as the pint of draught beer I had also ordered. My main thought now was whether I could eat the burger and drink the beer before my disapproving wife returned from the bank. If the bank was true to form then I should be okay, so I stopped panicking and returned to reading about Kremnica Castle.

'The dominant feature of the castle area is the late Gothic church of St. Katherine'. I read on and discovered that St. Katherine was also the patron saint of the town. She was a martyr who had been tortured and executed for her Christian beliefs, on a wheel of all things. It is for that reason that the Kremnica town shield has a half wheel on it, and not anything to do with mining as I had read in another guidebook, the previous night.

I suppose I was particularly interested in reading about St. Katherine, as she is also the patron saint of the church that I got married in. I had now gleaned some interesting wedding day related facts that I was sure would not fail to impress my wife, and with any luck draw attention away from a half-eaten burger if she came back from the bank too soon.

As I was thinking these devious thoughts, the waitress reappeared and presented me with a huge half-pound burger, drowning in Chilli Con Carne, together with a pint of Zlatý Bažant that had a frothy head resembling an ice-cream cone.

'Nech sa páči!' said the waitress, smiling.

"Thank you!" I said, wondering how I was going to manage to eat this giant in 10 minutes. "I mean, Ďakujem!"

I took a large mouthful of my burger, thinking what my father-in-law might say if he caught me eating this Western junk food. I then washed it down with a swig of beer and for the first time took in my surroundings.

I was in a medieval-style street, where all the little boutiques and cafés had old-fashioned, wooden signs, in keeping with the style. Directly ahead of me was Kremnica's town gate, and if it were not for the modern clothes of the people walking past and the Coca Cola signs, swaying in the breeze outside the cafés, it could have easily passed for another century.

If I stretched my neck out slightly, I could see Kremnica castle up on the hills in the distance. The sun was shining brightly from behind the castle and I shielded my eyes. I felt so relaxed. I was drinking one of the best lager beers that money can buy, and was half way through one of the biggest burgers I'd ever eaten. I sighed a contented sigh, and thought to myself... Hey, I could really get used to living in the heart of Europe.

From Morava With Love

A few weeks ago my wife and I borrowed my father-in-law's old, red Lada and drove across the Czech border to the town of Zlín, in Morava, to visit my wife's best friend, Veronika. She was actually staying with her parents for the summer, so this was a great opportunity for them to catch up on old times.

Ria and Veronika first met at college in England about four years ago and, despite the fact that the Czech and Slovak languages are so similar as to be perfectly understood by both, they have always insisted on speaking to each other only in English. This has always rather amused me, especially early on when they would prefer to struggle with phrases in English, rather than taking the easy option of conversing in their mother tongues.

This was my first visit to Zlín and indeed my first time in Morava. Many of Ria's friends and family had told me that the people of Morava were extremely friendly and had a very similar mentality to the Slovaks. I was soon to experience Moravan hospitality firsthand, as straight away we were made to feel very welcome by Veronika's family.

We were hardly through the door, when we were invited to the dinner table to try some typical Czech cuisine. Veronika's mother is an excellent cook and we soon tucked into a scrumptious meal. We were also introduced to a local red wine that Veronika's father had especially bought for the occasion. Both parents seemed to be very impressed at my level of Slovak, and to my surprise they understood me extremely well. I, on the other hand, found it very difficult to follow Czech, whereas a native Slovak would understand the language perfectly.

As the early evening progressed, we retired to the lounge and it wasn't long before plates of cheeses, hams, sausages and cakes were brought out to nibble on while we continued to drink the wine. This reminded me straight away of a typical scene when visiting relatives in Slovakia. You have just finished your evening meal and are now paying a visit to an auntie or uncle, when suddenly you are bombarded with a table full of snacks.

You make a feeble attempt to say that you can't possibly eat anything more but end up having to soldier on so as not to appear rude. As it turned out, in this particular case, it was lucky that the snacks were offered when they were, because they helped line my stomach for the incredible amount of alcohol I was about to consume that night.

As more and more glasses of wine were consumed, I began to get more of an ear for the Czech language and I began to decipher certain phrases, which from my perspective sounded like heavily accented Slovak that had been slightly mispronounced. Having seen how much I had enjoyed the Czech wine, our hosts decided that I should experience a tour of Zlín's Pubs, so that I could sample the many different Czech beers. I was told that there were a total of 77 pubs and bars in Zlín, which is an incredible number for such a small town. Our particular tour that evening consisted of seven pubs, where we enjoyed a different pint of the local brew in each one. The Czechs certainly enjoy their beer, more so even than the British, and I must confess that after all the wine I'd had I struggled to keep up the pace.

By this time of course I was very confident speaking Slovak, I was even speaking a little Czech. We talked, amongst other things, about the Velvet Revolution, the Velvet Divorce, the European Union and the up-and-coming General Elections in Slovakia. We also talked about the state of the economy, the exorbitant house prices in Great Britain, the Slovak rock group Elán and of course we talked about soccer.

All in all it was a really enjoyable night and a great start to the weekend. Needless to say we slept well that night, and didn't surface until late morning the following day. After eating a light lunch on the Saturday, we went into the town centre, where I vaguely recognized certain haunts from the night before. Zlín is a beautiful town, with a very unusual history. It is probably the only town in the Czech Republic that was not built around a castle or a market place. Zlín was built around a shoe factory.

In 1894, the son of a shoemaker, by the name of Tomáš Baťa, founded a shoe factory, which soon began attracting workers from the surrounding countryside. By the beginning of the 20th century there were about 3,000 inhabitants in the small town that rose up from the factory. Baťa then managed to secure the contract to supply the armies of the Habsburg Empire with their boots during the First World War. This meant that the factory was able to expand further and as it did so the town of Zlín grew. By 1930, Zlín had already grown to a population of more than 21,000, with Baťa having designed much of the town as a modern, working environment for his staff.

Baťa died in a plane crash in 1932 and the reigns of the factory were handed over to his son, also called Tomáš. When the Communists took power after the Second World War, the factory and shops were nationalized and so Tomáš Baťa Jr. went to Canada where he successfully built another factory town, Bataville, near Ottawa. Zlín, meanwhile, was renamed Gottwaldov, after Czechoslovakia's first Communist president, Klement Gottwald. The Baťa shoe factory was also renamed; now it was called Svit.

The Baťa legacy is still very much evident today. This is especially so with regards to the simple, square-shaped, red brick houses, which Baťa constructed to house his workers. Many of these houses remain in Zlín, and are some of the best accommodation in the town. It was in one of the Baťa built houses that we found ourselves that Saturday evening, visiting Veronika's auntie and uncle. We sat out in the garden, enjoying a wonderful summer evening, talking, laughing, drinking wine, and of course eating a never ending supply of snacks.

So it was with much reluctance that we left Zlín, early on Sunday morning, and headed back for Slovakia. Veronika's family gathered round to wave us goodbye, and as we drove off I noticed that her father had his camera with him. The reason for this, as I later found out, was that he did not want to miss the opportunity to take a photo of an Englishman driving away in a 25 year old Lada. We would certainly miss Morava.

Easter Traditions

Although my wife and I have spent many a Christmas with her family, until this year we had yet to spend the Easter holidays together in Slovakia. I hadn't really given much thought to this, until a conversation I had with my father-in-law back in October of last year.

It was then, over a couple of pints of Pilsner in the local krčma, that I first learned of the Easter Monday tradition of keeping women 'fresh' for the coming year. With my limited Slovak, I was able to get the gist of what the tradition was all about, and by the expression on his face it was obviously a time of the year that he very much enjoyed. Later that evening, I probed my wife for more information and found that she was not very forthcoming. However, I eventually learned why we had never before spent Easter in Slovakia.

My wife explained that the Easter Monday tradition involved women getting buckets of water thrown over them and, if that wasn't enough, getting beat with a stick made from willow. In return, the women, no doubt grateful that they had been made fresh again, gave the men glasses of schnapps, chocolate, sweets, money and decorated eggs.

My wife also explained that under no circumstances would we be joining in with this tradition and that she would be making herself scarce come Easter. Although I must confess I liked the idea of lots of women serving me with schnapps and chocolate, I did think that beating women with a willow branch and soaking them to the skin with water a bit much, and so agreed that we would go away somewhere for the Easter week-end.

* * *

Easter came so early this year, that it was suddenly upon us before we knew what was what. We still hadn't made any definite plans to go away for the weekend by the middle of March, so by and by I convinced my wife that we should spend Easter with her parents. Eventually she agreed and even said that I could join in the Easter Monday traditions, on the strict understanding that on no account was she to get wet.

Spring had well and truly arrived by Easter Saturday in Slovakia. The sun was shining brightly and we enjoyed a lovely weekend, which included long walks, cooking gulàš over an open fire, and basking in the unexpected sunshine. On Sunday afternoon, Ria and her mum made cakes and decorated eggs, in preparation for the next day.

I was woken up early on Easter Monday morning by the screams of my wife. Looking up I saw my father-in-law, dressed in his best suit, with a half-empty cup of water and a wide grin on his face. Behind him my mother-in-law, who looked like she had just taken a shower with her clothes on, was also grinning. Looking now at my wife, I realized that she had received nothing more than a token sprinkle of water, but to hear her you would have thought that her father had drenched her with all the waters of the Danube.

I got dressed and had a hearty breakfast, before setting out with Ria's father at 8am, in search of other female members of the family to freshen, and to collect our schnapps and chocolate eggs. Meanwhile, Ria and her mum stayed indoors, awaiting the various uncles and cousins, who would be calling on them during the day.

Ria has a big family and by midday we must have visited about seven households in all. This meant that a lot of schnapps had been consumed, as well as countless cakes, sweets and savory nick-nacks that were placed out before us when we called.

There was no whipping of women with willow sticks, and my father-in-law and I only indulged in the cursory spraying of water and perfume.... honestly! However, we were presented with lots of decorated eggs, chocolate eggs and of course schnapps, plenty of schnapps.

In the end, the day turned out to be a lot different to how my wife had described it to me. What I experienced was a wonderful tradition, where the family was able to get together and talk, laugh, drink, eat and have some fun. That said, both

Ria's sisters were nowhere to be found that day, and my wife herself had mysteriously come down with a cold, much to the annoyance of her cousins and uncles.

The Gateway To The Tatras

Shading my eyes from the bright sunlight, I peered ahead at the horizon. Towering over a forest of fir trees, pale gray mountains rose up majestically, piercing the deep blue sky above. Most striking of all was the peak of Mount Kriváň, the unusual shape of which had caught my eye as I enjoyed my first glimpse of the High Tatras.

"Ria, you can see why it's called the curved mountain!" I called out to my wife, who had crossed over to the other side of the road, so that the passing cars would not spoil the photos she was taking.

"It's beautiful, isn't it!" she called back, as she tried again to capture the view on our digital camera.

We were parked in a lay-by on the E50 road, a chance to stretch our legs and to take in our surroundings. We were heading for Poprad, the so-called 'Gateway to the Tatras', and this would be as close as we'd get to the High Tatras for the time being, as we planned to go East from there, and see what Eastern Slovakia had to offer. So we intended to make the most of this photo opportunity and take some nice pictures.

"That's about as good as I can get it," exclaimed Ria, having crossed back over the road, and showed me the pictures she had taken on the camera's viewer. "The light's not too good, because the sun is ahead of us."

As I stood viewing the different shots of Krivan, a car pulled in to the lay-by and parked behind us. A young couple and two children bundled out and looked off into the direction of the mountains. By the number plates of the car I could see that they were Czech.

Crossing the road myself, I tried my hand at taking some photos. Though I knew that it would be impossible to fully capture what we saw ahead of us on film, especially with my rather limited camera, I still fancied I'd fare rather better than my wife's efforts. However, after a few attempts I realized that this was not the case and, dejectedly, I crossed back over to the car.

Meanwhile, my wife had struck up a conversation with the Czech couple, whom it turned out were heading for Štrbské Pleso, a popular resort in the Tatras, set around a mountain lake of the same name. She was now looking through a pair of powerful binoculars that the Czech guy had lent her, gazing up at the mountains ahead.

"Wow, these are amazing! You can see everything so clearly. Here, have a look," she said, passing the binoculars to me.

I looked at the Czech guy, half apologetically, but he nodded his approval so I held the binoculars up to my eyes and focused in on Mount Kriváň.

Mount Kriváň stands at 2,494 meters, in the western part of the High Tatras. It was once thought by the Liptov locals to be the highest mountain in the whole of the Tatras range, a fact hotly disputed by the people from Spiš, who claimed that their nearby Lomnický štít was actually the highest peak. This debate went on for many a year until the technology finally arrived that could prove once and for all which of the mountains was the highest in the Tatras.

The results came as a bit of a shock to both camps, as it turned out that Gerlachovský štít, at 2,654 meters, was in fact the highest peak. However, the Spiš locals did get some satisfaction with the fact that at 2,634 meters, Lomnický štít was an incredible 140 meters higher than its rival.

Although it may not be the highest of the Tatra Mountains, there is little doubt that it is the most intriguing. "Kriváň" means "curved" in the Slovak language and there is a wonderful legend behind how the mountain got its unusual shape. The story goes thus:

When God created the earth he was generally pleased with what he had achieved, but he decided that he would add some more beauty to various places, all around the world. So he sent forth his angels into the world with an enormous sack, which held this beauty within, with orders to distribute the contents evenly throughout the lands. However, as the angels passed over one particular mountain, they misjudged its height, and the sack was torn on its peak.

This resulted in the contents of the sack spilling out over the region surrounding the mountain. Mountains, valleys, rivers, forests, waterfalls, lakes all spilled out over the land below; bears, deer, chamois and many other animals also leapt out from the sack. Meanwhile, the peak that had torn the sack had been permanently curved by the impact.

So now you know the reason why Mount Kriváň is curved, and why the High Tatras has so many natural beauties in such a small area.

Having thanked the couple for the loan of their binoculars, we took one last look at Kriváň and got into the car. The next time we would see the curved mountain would be at the end of our journey. We set off once more and headed for Poprad.

* * *

Don't get me wrong, it's not that I particularly dislike Poprad; I suppose I just expected more... a whole lot more. When your town is situated at the foot of one of the most spectacular natural phenomenon in Europe, and indeed you market your town as 'The Gateway to the Tatras', you wouldn't expect ... well let's just say you wouldn't expect Poprad. Perhaps I am being a little harsh on Poprad, but let's just say we didn't exactly hit it off from the word go.

Having arrived in Poprad and having parked the car near the town square, we headed off for the hotel district, which was about a ten-minute walk from the center, in order to find a place to spend the night. You see we hadn't bothered to reserve any hotels, as it was not the high season, and also because we wanted to find out what were the best deals when we got there.

Of course, if there happens to be a national medical conference taking place in a town that only has about six hotels to its name, it doesn't really matter whether it's high season or not. Everywhere we tried was fully booked. We went from hotel to hotel, stepping down in class as we went, but at each one we got the same response - no room at the inn. What it did give us, however, was a chance to view all the hotels that Poprad has to offer.

Apart from one extortionately high-priced hotel, aimed at business cliental rather than the tourist, all the hotels that we went to resembled office blocks. Many of these we passed by at first, thinking that's exactly what they were, until we saw a sign announcing that it was in fact a hotel after all. However, what each of these hotels did offer was a tremendous view of the Tatras, and so I would have accepted the higher than normal prices, and indeed would have stayed at any of them, if they had not been full.

We of course were now presented with a problem - where to spend the night? However, this was a problem that we decided to put off for a while, as it was already lunchtime and we were both famished.

If the hotels of Poprad are not the most appealing in the world, the same cannot be said about the restaurants, well certainly not the first bistro that we happened upon once the hunger pangs had set in. The Egidius, situated opposite one of the office block-hotels, was a delight. It was a quaint wooden affair, with three floors, the third of which had a balcony looking out over the mountains. The food was also splendid, plenty of it and with a nice choice of draught beer to wash it down with.

Having ate our fill, we flicked through the guidebooks and printouts from various web sites, as we contemplated what we would do concerning the hotel situation. It was soon decided that we would spend the afternoon in Poprad's town square, visiting the various tourist attractions on offer. Then in the evening, we would make for the small town of Spišská Sobota, on the outskirts of Poprad; if we were fortunate enough to find a hotel room that is.

Before we left the Egidius, I went out onto the balcony to finish my beer and to gaze once more at the mountains. The sun had gone in behind some clouds and the sky had turned overcast, spoiling what would have been a perfect view. Looking at the mountains and then at the line of office-block hotels to my left, it struck me that Poprad really was on a hiding to nothing. In a different setting these hotels, the other buildings and the town itself would have appeared to be ordinary and nothing worse, but here, in contrast with their idyllic setting, they were just plain ugly.

As we left the Egidius, and made our way to the town square, my wife spied a bank up ahead.

"Shall we change some of our traveler's checks?" she asked. "By the time we pay out for the hotel and have something to eat tonight we'll be running low on cash."

"Okay, we might as well change them here, as it is convenient," I answered, thinking nothing of it. "But we had better be quick as we haven't got all that much time to see the museum and the gallery."

We entered the bank at five minutes past two in the afternoon.

It has always amused me when we change up traveler's checks in Ria's hometown, that such a simple transaction, which should really only take a couple of minutes, can take anything up to twenty minutes to complete. It seems that there is an unspoken rule in Slovakia; why let one person do a job, when three people can do it just as well. In our local Slovak bank there is someone to check your signature, someone to work out how much money you should get and then finally after a compulsory ten minute wait, someone to count your money out and give it to you. It used to bother me a little when I first arrived in Slovakia, but now that I know I'm in for a quarter of an hour wait, I simply make myself comfortable in one of the bank's black leather armchairs and bide my time.

Of course, this wouldn't be the case in a bank in Poprad, the "Gateway to the Tatras", it would probably just take a few minutes and we could be on our way. What is more there were no other customers in the bank, and about five cashiers waiting to serve. We approached the nearest cashier and my wife placed $100 worth of checks, together with her passport on the counter.

The friendly smile of the young cashier quickly vanished as she saw the traveler's checks placed in front of her. After examining them for a while, she looked up, whispered "Moment!" and went off for help.

"Trust us to get someone on their first day!" I laughed to my wife. But even as I said this, I knew that this probably wasn't the case.

After a few minutes the cashier returned with an older lady, presumably the manager of the bank, who took the two traveler's checks in her hand and examined them for a full two minutes, before finally looking up at us and then back at the checks again. Then after a while longer she muttered "Moment!" and walked over to another colleague who was sat at a table at the back of the bank.

Together the two ladies poured over the traveler's checks, talking quietly to themselves, and shortly a third lady joined them. Presently, the third lady went away from the table, in order to fetch a big black folder from a nearby shelf and then returned to the table, where the three women proceeded to use the folder as a point of reference.

At first I was transfixed by what was going on, but unable to contain myself any longer, I finally questioned my wife, loud enough so that the young cashier could hear.

"What the hell are they doing?" I said.

"I don't think they have seen this make of traveler's check before," answered my wife.

"What! It's the most popular make of traveler's check there is!" I continued. "This is supposed to be one of the main tourist hubs in Slovakia, this is the "Gateway to the Tatras", are you trying to tell me they've never seen a traveler's check before?"

"No, just not this make that's all," whispered my wife, concerned no doubt that I might be making a scene. "Why don't you go and sit down over there!"

Taking my wife's suggestion on board, I went and sat down on a bench on the other side of the room, to cool down. Eventually, I took one of the guidebooks out of my backpack and started reading about Poprad.

Amongst other things, I learnt that Poprad, with its population of over 55,000, is actually one of the ten largest towns in Slovakia. It is also the administrative capital of the Tatras region. There are a number of roads into the town, linking it to all the major cities in the area and it also has its own airport.

Poprad lies on an important railway line, which apparently was the main factor for the rapid growth of the town, in the late C19th. Up until then, the neighboring town of Spišská Sobota was in fact the largest and most populated town in the area.

Due to its position, at the foot of the Tatra Mountain range, Poprad obviously enjoys a good tourist trade. Tens of thousands of tourists, both from Slovakia and abroad, pass through Poprad on their way to the mountains each year, and many others use the town as a base to explore the Upper Spiš region.

"I wonder how many of those tourists needed to change up traveler's checks?" I thought to myself, and looking over to my wife I could see that she was still waiting patiently by the counter. I got up from my seat and joined her.

"Look, we've been waiting for over half an hour, this is ridiculous!" I reasoned with my wife. "What are they doing now?"

"They are phoning head office," said my wife, and sighed. "What time is it?"

"It's ten to three! We probably won't be able to go to the art gallery now," I exclaimed. "Can't you say something?"

"I have. They said that they haven't done one of these before and that they need to ring up the head office or something," whispered my wife, in a tone that warned me not to say anything more.

Just then the senior woman returned with the two traveler's checks, whispered something to the young cashier and then left. The smile now returned to the cashier's face - Head Office had given the okay! Then the checks were signed and the exchange rate was worked out, the compulsory ten minute wait was observed and finally the money was counted out and given to us.

We left the bank at ten minutes past three in the afternoon.

During the hour or so that we had spent in the bank, the sun had come back out, and it took us a while to adjust to the brightness. The sunlight now lit up the mountains, and we could see the snow capped peaks for miles around. I quickly forgot the frustration of the bank and suddenly felt really good.

"Come on," I said to my wife. "Let's see what the Podtatranské Museum has to offer."

At first we were not too sure whether the Podtatranské museum was open or not. The door was locked and there didn't appear to be any lights on in the building. On closer inspection, we saw a little sign above the doorbell requesting that you should ring the bell once; so we did.

Presently, we heard the unbolting of many locks, the door then opened and a middle-aged woman beckoned us in. We apologized for disturbing her and asked her if the museum was open. She looked at us as if we were a little stupid, of course the museum was open, and she led us to the ticket office so that we could pay the 20Sk entrance fee.

Founded in 1886, and one of the oldest museums in Slovakia, the Podtatranské museum currently holds the superb 'Gánovce Exposition'. This is an exhibition that presents the life and environment of a Neanderthal man, who lived in the region about 100,000 years ago.

The 'Gánovce Exposition' is the only one of its type in Slovakia, and came about because of the discovery of the skull of a Neanderthal man in the nearby village of Gánovce. This is in fact the earliest example of people living in Slovakia. The skull itself can be found in a museum in Prague, but there is a molding of the skull present, which takes center stage in the museum. Most of the other exhibits, such as bones from Mammoths and pre-historic cave bears, are all originals and were actually discovered in the Poprad region.

Although it was a bit on the small side, I found the 'Gánovce Exposition' extremely interesting, and was able to read about each of the exhibits from a photocopied booklet that the curator had kindly presented me with, when she discovered I was English.

Having absorbed a wealth of information about a day in the life of a Neanderthal man, we were then shown to the other exposition that is housed in the museum. This was an archaeological exhibition, with relics and finds through the ages from the Stone Age to Celtic and Roman times. This was interesting enough, but it is Gánovce Man that makes the museum well worth the admission fee.

By the time we left the museum it was past four o'clock, so we found a phone box and Ria managed to make a reservation at a pension in Spišská Sobota. We didn't really know what to expect from the town, as very little was written about it in the guidebooks. We just wanted to secure a place to spend the night, and get something to eat. We found the car, and made our way to Spišská Sobota, feeling a little tired now as the day drew to a close.

*   *   *

Occasionally, on your travels, you are lucky enough to stumble upon a real gem of a place. A town, a hotel, or perhaps an attraction, that far exceeds your expectations. This was one such time for us.

We had booked in to the Penzión Fortuna, in Spišská Sobota, just before five, had freshened ourselves up in our room and had enjoyed a good meal in the restaurant. We had managed to reserve their luxury apartment, which consisted of two floors and had a nice view of the main square. The first floor included a living room with a fireplace, and a bathroom with a whirlpool bath. On the second floor was a comfortable sleeping area. All this for less than $60. I was extremely thankful to the doctors of Slovakia for having had their medical conference in Poprad.

At just past seven o'clock, we decided to take a stroll around the town square, to walk off our supper. It was getting dark and it was eerily quiet, with not a soul about.

The cobbled main square in Spišská Sobota is a peculiar, triangular shape, which is lined with pastel colored Burgher houses. Most of these Burgher houses have been fully renovated, so that they look as good as new, and many of them are now pensions or restaurants. However, a few of the houses had seemingly been left untouched for half a century or more, and are near ruins, which seemed to add to the solitude.

As we slowly walked along the street I took in my surroundings. Except for the three cars parked in the center, I doubt if the square would have looked much different one hundred and fifty years before. I tried to imagine the bustle of people going about their business when this was the main town in the whole of the Tatra region. Now, it was just so peaceful.

Suddenly, one by one, Victorian-style street lamps lit up all around the square. At the same time the centerpiece of the town, the Roman Catholic Church of St. Juraj, came alive with bright lights, which lit up the sky above.

Stars twinkled around the church spire and a full moon, which had been hidden by a cloud, now came out and shone down on the square, bringing out the vibrant colors of the Burgher houses below. Ria and I looked at each other and smiled.

"What a wonderful night!" she sighed.

Making Sausages

I had been invited along to watch Vlado, and his team of assistants, skillfully make sausages in the traditional way. I was told that I could report on each stage of the sausage making process, on the strict understanding that I would not disclose any of the secret ingredients that are added to make, what Vlado describes as, “the best sausages in the world”.

So there I was one winter morning, in a freezing cold garage in a tiny little village somewhere in Orava, armed with notepad and pen, eagerly awaiting a lesson in how to make Slovak sausages.

The first stage, as with any recipe, was the preparation of the ingredients. The pork had been purchased earlier that morning, and the herbs and spices were packed in their individual containers, ready for weighing. A bottle of whiskey was also present, but it turned out that this would not form part of the secret ingredients that gave the sausages their distinct flavor. Pride of place amongst all the different spices, that would eventually be added to the pork mixture, was a 1lb bag of paprika. I gathered from the oohs and ahhs that filled the room when Vlado placed it on the table that this was pretty good stuff.

Once Vlado was satisfied all the ingredients were correctly weighed, we indulged in our first whiskey of the day. Although it was only about 11 o' clock in the morning, the whiskey was a welcome sight, as it was 14 degrees Fahrenheit outside, and to be frank it wasn't much warmer inside the garage. Having made a toast to "Good sausages!", I was then introduced to the mincer. This was an electrically powered monstrosity from the 1940's, but was still in perfect working order and the mincing began with half a pound of garlic. So with a warm feeling in my stomach, from the whiskey, and the beautiful aroma of minced garlic filling the garage, I felt really relaxed and ready to start making some sausages.

After the garlic had worked its way through the mincer it was the turn of the meat. The pork was certainly not the best cut of meat I've seen in my life, but then we were making sausages, not steaks. Even so, quite a bit of fat needed to be removed, so that the mincer did not get blocked. However, I noticed that the less stringy bits of fat still made they way, along with the meat, into the tub below. Having worked its way through the mincer, the minced meat landed in a big blue bath tub. This continued until there was no meat (or usable fat) left, and the bath tub was three quarters full. At this point in the proceedings, Vlado decided that we had earned a break and so out came the whiskey bottle once more, and another toast was made.

The next stage was to mix the mince up. This was done by hand, in the same way as you would knead dough for bread. I was asked if I would like to have a go. It looked messy, but I thought I'd better show willing, so I agreed. It was messy, and surprisingly cold. After doing my bit for a few minutes I let the experts take over, and wondered how long it would be until the next whiskey.

Now things began to spice up (if you'll pardon the pun). About 10 different herbs and spices were added to the minced meat, as well as some sugar. Now if you remember, I had sworn that I would not write about specific ingredients, but if the truth be told I didn't recognize most of them anyway. Once all the herbs and spices had been added, it was time for some more mixing.

Did I say all the herbs and spices? Not quite all, there were still the secret ingredients, including that special paprika, to be added, which when mixed together made a thick, dark red sauce. Once this sauce had slowly been poured out into the blue tub below, Vlado signaled that it was time for another break. Perhaps this pause was due to the fact that we were ready for our third whiskey of the morning, but I think it is more likely that he just wanted us to take the time to marvel at his beautiful sauce before it was mixed in.

Now that all the ingredients had been added (even the secret ones) it was back once more to some serious mixing. This continued until the sauce had been totally soaked up by the mince. The mixture was now ready to be fed into the sausage making machine, which had been taken out of a cupboard and was being assembled next to the mincer. However, before we could begin to load the sausage maker, we first needed to form the mince into big round balls, about the size of a fist.

While the sausage making machine was being assembled and the mince balls were being made, the whiskey bottle reappeared once more. Looking at the sausage machine, I felt that it resembled a silver sausage gun. It worked on the principle that three or four of the pre-made mince balls were loaded in at the top end of the gun, and then a handle was turned until the sausage meat began to shoot out at the bottom end. Before we could begin this process though, something had to be added at the bottom of the sausage gun to shoot the sausage meat into.

I had been wondering all morning what the little bowl of water next to the mincer was for, and now as Vlado proceeded to take some stringy, opaque substance out of the bowl, it suddenly dawned on me. This was the pig's intestine that would act as the sausage's skin, and which was now skillfully wrapped around the bottom end of the gun. Then the handle was slowly turned, and the sausage meat shot out of the gun into the skin, forming a long sausage, which wrapped itself round and round into a spiral, until the skin was completely filled. I noticed that I wasn't asked if I would like to help at this particular stage, as this was obviously skilled work that had been mastered over many years.

Once the skin was completely filled, the spiral of sausage meat was then separated out into about seven large sausages. This was done by twisting the sausage at various points, in a sort of skipping rope action. It was done with such deft of hand and so quickly, that it was made to look quite easy, but I could imagine what my efforts would have turned out like, if I had been allowed to have a go.

The loading of mince balls, the squirting of sausage meat, and the twisting of the sausages continued until we had filled a large bucket full with sausages. Our reward was a fifth whiskey, and we made a toast to a good morning's work.

All that was left to do now was to hang the sausages up in an outdoor oven, which actually had a chimney, so that they could be smoked for three days.

And just so you know, I can confirm that Vlado was quite right, they were the best sausages in the world. Well, the best that I have ever tasted anyway.

World Champions

It was the night of the 11th May, 2002, a night to remember, and a night when the Slovak Nation celebrated as one. The national team had defeated Russia 4-3 in the final of the Ice Hockey World Championships in Gothenburg, and Slovakia, for the first time in their nine-year history, had become world champions. What a night to be in Slovakia, with town squares up and down the country full of jubilant people, young and old, partying until late into the night.

I would have loved to have soaked up the joyous atmosphere in the nation's capital, as thousands flocked to the SNP square, waving flags, singing victory songs, and saluting Peter Bondra, Miroslav Šatan, Ján Lašák, and the rest of their magnificent heroes.

Of course, as circumstances would have it, I wasn't in Slovakia at all that night. Instead, my wife and I had an early night in, at a fine hotel, in a quiet Czech spa town close to the border with Germany.

* * *

I don't think I had ever watched an Ice Hockey match before I saw Slovakia's first game against Poland, in the preliminary group stages. You see Ice Hockey isn't really played in the UK, perhaps it is because there's not enough snow there, but anyway whatever the reason it's about as popular as cricket is in the States. However, by the time Slovakia had safely reached the knockout phase of the tournament, Ice Hockey had a new British fan, I was well and truly hooked.

As I didn't know a powerplay from a face-off, the first couple of games were spent trying to fathom the rules. My father-in-law diligently tried to explain them to me, and despite my poor Slovak, I soon picked them up. What I found more difficult though was keeping pace with the puck. I was convinced that the Slovak commentator must see the game a few seconds in advance, as he would often shout "goal", while I was still lost down the other end of the pitch. By and by my eyes became accustomed to the speed, and by the second period of the second game against Finland, I pretty much knew what was going on.

It was about this time that I witnessed my first Ice Hockey fight. It was a fully-fledged fist fight that, had it been a soccer match, would have seen the two participants banned from the sport for a season or two. I was quite amazed to find that bashing the living daylights out of your opponent only warrants a 14-minute penalty in the sport of Ice Hockey. Unfortunately, it was our star player, Peter Bondra, who was penalized, and without him for 14 minutes of the game, Slovakia ended up losing their second match of the tournament to Finland, by 3 goals to 1.

As it turned out, the loss to Finland would be the only loss of the tournament for Slovakia, who then proceeded to soundly beat Ukraine, Sweden and Russia in the remaining qualifying games. So on to the knockout stages, where Slovakia would face Canada, one of the pre-tournament favorites.

Now that things were getting more exciting, it wasn't just my father-in-law and I that watched the match, but the whole family, and we now watched it in our local hostinec, on a big screen. This was to soak up the atmosphere, for what we realistically thought would be Slovakia's final game. The quarterfinal against Canada was superb, probably the most exciting of the whole tournament. Although playing the better hockey, Slovakia soon found herself two goals to nil down to the reigning Olympic champions.

The locals within the hostinec were not at all pleased with their team, the opposition team and, in particular, the referee, and I certainly learnt a few new Slovak expletives that night. However, towards the end of the second period, when most of us were resigned to the fact that we were going to lose, Peter Bondra suddenly performed some inspirational play, culminating in the goal of the tournament. With the score at 2-1, with twenty minutes to play, Slovakia were still in with a chance. The final period of the game was tense to say the least.

Slovakia's captain, Miroslav Šatan, scored a fine goal to bring the game level, and then Bondra scored again, to give Slovakia the advantage. A late surge by Canada at the end of the game was not enough, and so Slovakia came out the victors by three goals to two.

Slovakia were through to the semi-finals against the hosts, Sweden. Again Slovakia were the underdogs, but again after an almighty struggle they won through. This time it was even closer, going all the way to penalties. I remember the complete silence as Slovakia prepared to take the deciding penalty. I was willing them to score, but couldn't bear to look. Suddenly, a crescendo of noise filled the hostinec, and that could mean only one thing. All around me people were jumping up and down, screaming, shouting in delight; hugging each other, friends, family and complete strangers. Slovakia had done it; they had made it to the final.

* * *

When my wife and I made our plans for the 11th May, I had no idea that there would be an Ice Hockey Championship in full swing, let alone that Slovakia would be in the final. So it was with great regret that we set off from Slovakia on that Saturday morning, and we were determined that we would some how get the chance to watch the game.

We had planned to drive to Germany and spend the night there, but we could not guarantee that the final would be on German television, so we stopped for the night in Teplice instead, just short of the Czech/German border. In Teplice, we found a wonderful little hotel, which we booked into, then quickly got showered and changed, before setting off in search of a place that was showing the game. We were both extremely hungry, so we were pleased to find a pizzeria close by that was showing the final on a big screen. As well as showing the hockey, they also had ice-cold Pilsner on tap. This should be a good night, I thought.

I was half way through my first pint of Pilsner, when the match began. By this time a number of Czechs had crowded around the bar area, settling down to watch the game as well. When the Slovak team came out on to the pitch, the Czechs all began to cheer, they had obviously adopted Slovakia for the night. I tried to imagine being in a pub in Scotland, with a crowd of Scots cheering on England in the soccer World Cup Finals, and smiled.

It wasn't too long before the Czechs and I had something to cheer about. Slovakia scored the first goal, and then a second to make it 2-0. Then Miroslav Šatan had a third goal cruelly disallowed, it seemed plain sailing for the Slovaks. I sat back and relaxed and enjoyed my beer, this will be easy I thought. I was wrong. Into the second period, and on to my second pint of Pilsner, Russia struck back with a goal. However, Slovakia soon maintained the two goal advantage, with a fine goal by Miroslav Šatan to make it 3-1. I was now enjoying my pizza, and the thoughts that my adopted country would soon be World Champions. I only hoped that England could match this feat in the up-and-coming soccer tournament during the summer.

Of course, my celebrations were somewhat premature. The Canada and Sweden games had been on the edge of your seat stuff, and the final was to be no different. Russia began to play much better hockey in the third period, and scored a second and then a third goal, to make it all square, at three a piece. With barely six minutes left to play, it was anybody's game. By now the play was flowing, and so was the beer. I was well into my fourth Pilsner, when Peter Bondra scored Slovakia's fourth, and the games deciding goal.

A huge cheer went up in the pizzeria, there was only a minute left to go, surely Slovakia would win now. That final minute seemed to drag on for ages, and then finally the hooter went to sound the end of the match. Slovakia had become World Champions!

Loud cheers from the Czechs now filled the pizzeria, but the loudest cheer of all was from an Englishman, who had perhaps had one Pilsner too many.

Kežmarok and Levoča: A Tale Of Two Cities

My wife and I were looking at our various guide books and internet printouts, making plans for our weekend trip to the Spiš region, in Eastern Slovakia.

"We'll probably spend most of the day in Kežmarok," I reasoned with my wife. "There seems to be quite a lot to do there."

"Okay, but we'll spend the night in Levoča," replied Ria. "So I should really phone now and reserve a hotel. We might not be able to find a decent one at the last minute."

We finally agreed on a hotel in Levoča, choosing a mid-range one, as the luxury hotels seemed to be a bit more pricey than in many of the other towns in the region. Once the hotel was booked and we were satisfied that everything was packed, we began our journey to Kežmarok.

Located on an important trade route, connecting north Europe with the Orient, Kežmarok received the status of a free royal city in 1380 and was quite prosperous during the 15th and 16th centuries. At this time, there were almost 40 town guilds, with masters and apprentices making everything from fishing nets to clocks. The town was particularly well known for its goldsmiths, carpenters and blue-dyers.

Kežmarok was also involved in many wars throughout the centuries. One of the most long-standing was the conflict with their neighbors, Levoča, over the rights to storage, which lasted over 100 years. Another long running dispute that Kežmarok experienced, was one between the castle and the town. Originally built to protect Kežmarok, the owners of the castle decided that they would prefer to rule over the town themselves. This led to armed clashes between the townspeople and the castle soldiers for almost 250 years. Finally though, it was the town that won the day, when they actually bought the castle from the last owner, in 1702.

From Kežmarok, we would be going on to Levoča, a town that I was really looking forward to visiting. Looking at the map, there did not appear to be a road linking the two towns. Instead, we would have to double back on ourselves to Poprad, before then heading east to Levoča.

We arrived in Kežmarok at half-past nine, but already the sun was shining brightly. We parked the car on the outskirts of town, not far from the two Protestant churches that together formed one of Kežmarok's main tourist attractions. The two churches, standing side by side, were in complete contrast to each other. The first church was a small, simple affair, made entirely from wood. The second, a grand, bright orange building, which had the appearance of a small cathedral.

I thought that the two churches looked quite odd standing there together, so far from the town center. I learnt later that there was a reason for this. Kežmarok, historically a Roman Catholic town, had quite strict rules on the building of Protestant churches. Firstly, the church had to be built outside of the town walls, and then on a precisely marked spot. Secondly, the church could only be paid for by the Protestant parish, which was typically quite poor. For this reason, early Protestant churches in Slovakia were made of wood, the cheapest material available.

As we locked the car, a man came trundling over to us. He was quite small, but with an enormous beer belly, and in his hands he had what looked like a book of lottery tickets.

"How long please?" he asked in pigeon English.

My wife replied in Slovak that we would probably be staying for most of the day.

"40 korona please. You have secure parking!" he stated, persevering with his English.

We paid him the money and received about a dozen of the lottery tickets to place inside the windscreen. Checking all the valuables were out of the car, I tested that each of the doors were securely locked, and then joined my wife, who was already walking towards the churches. I looked back to see that the small, fat man had been joined by a tall, skinny guy. Both appeared to be looking into our car.

"I'm not too happy about parking the car there," I confessed to my wife.

"Relax!" said my wife. "It's secure parking!"

"It's the people doing the securing that I'm worried about!" I argued, looking back again, relieved to see that they had turned their attention to another car.

"Come on, let's get you to church," she said, grinning.

Unfortunately, neither of the churches were open. We tried the imposing New Evangelical church first, but the iron doors were locked and there was a small sign saying that the church was in fact closed for the day. The less than impressive wooden articular church, next door, was also closed, but at least that was open to the public in the afternoon. We decided to make our way to the Tourist Information Center and then begin our sightseeing from the town square. We could always pop into the church on the way back to the car, if we had time before going on to Levoča.

Kežmarok's Hlavné námestie, or Main Square, was quite small, but with a number of different architectural styles. We passed a number of interesting buildings; such as the gothic Town Hall and the renaissance style Redoute, before happening upon the tourist center. Here, the staff were exceptionally helpful, handing us a number of free information leaflets and pointing out that the next guided tour of the castle would be at 11.00 am.

This was in complete contrast to our experience at the Poprad tourist center, when we had visited the "Gateway to the Tatras". There we had received a few grunts from the less than helpful staff, and had ended up paying a small fortune on leaflets and pamphlets for the information we required.

Kežmarok had a tourist center that provided you with information and a smile, which immediately made you feel good about the town. Remarkably, they even gave us a bag, to put our leaflets in, and for free. I had never been given a bag in Slovakia before, not even in a grocery store, without specifically asking for one and then paying for it. I was impressed.

Our first port of call was the castle, where we received a free postcard with our entrance tickets and what's more the tour was conducted in English, and for the next hour I enjoyed what has got to be one of the most interesting tourist attractions in Slovakia.

We began the tour on the first floor of the castle, with an exhibition covering the history of Kežmarok. The first part was about the different guilds that were set up in the town, from the C15th onwards. There had been a total of 37 independent guilds active, including locksmiths, fisherman, tanners, spinners, stonecutters and masons. Examples of their skilled crafts, as well as each guild's standards, plaques and seals were on display behind glass cabinets.

Our guide explained that each guild consisted of closed craftsmen associations that were governed by very strict rules, known as "articles". Each guild had three levels of expertise - Apprentice, Journeyman and Master. An Apprentice began by learning his particular trade from a Master.

Then when he was ready, usually after a few years, he would become a Journeyman and travel round the country plying his trade and gaining experience. After a specified length of time, between two to ten years, depending on the guild, the Journeyman would be allowed to sit his exams to become a Master. However, success in the exams was not the only pre-requisite to becoming a Master. The Journeyman would also have to be able to afford to pay the set fees to the guild chest. For this reason there were always many skilled and experienced Journeymen who, because they were poor, never quite made it to the level of Master.

From the Guilds and Crafts exposition, we crossed through into another room, which was the first floor of a tower. Here we found the first stage of an exposition showing the development of weapons from the Middle Ages up until the C19th. Each floor of the tower presented a different stage of a collection of C15th to C17th armor and arms. This included swords, daggers, sabers, maces and pickaxes, from Hungary, Germany, Austria and the Orient.

The exhibits also included two swords, which were crossed to form a large X, displayed on the wall of the tower. One sword had a red handle, while the other had a black one. The guide explained to us that these swords were used in the past as a warning signal to the people living in the town, placed in front of the castle during times of danger. The red-handled sword would be used to warn that an enemy was coming to attack the town, while the black-handled sword warned people that the dreaded Plague had hit the town. From what I had read earlier about the town's history, the red-handled sword had certainly seen the light of day on numerous occasions.

From the top of the tower, we passed along the castle wall where we could see out over the turrets to a view of the surrounding countryside. We carried along the wall until we reached another tower, and yet another exhibition. This one was dedicated to the Kežmarok Shooters' Union, unsurprisingly the only one of its type in Slovakia. The Shooters' Union was founded in 1510, and had a similar structure to the town's guilds. It continued up until the Second World War, when it was then disbanded.

On display, we could see various targets and prizes from competitions spanning the 400 years that the Union was in existence. I noticed that the writing on the targets and prizes was in German, as this was the written language at that time, when Slovakia was still part of the Kingdom of Hungary. I also noticed that most of the early targets exhibited had very few bullet holes in them. Our guide explained that the early guns were so primitive that a direct hit was usually more by luck than judgment.

The next two rooms we went to housed the Exposition of the Association of Spiš Physicians and Apothecaries, which was my personal favorite exhibition in the castle. The first room was a mock up of a pharmacy from the C19th. Every little detail of the pharmacy was so authentic that you could easily imagine what it would have been like going for a prescription 150 years ago. There were black cabinets, with little drawers containing various types of herbs, as well as bottles of medicines, drugs and poisons (with their distinctive white writing on black labels). There was also a display of the typical medical instruments from that period, such as syringes, stethoscopes and surgical knives.

The second room was a reconstruction of the consulting room belonging to one of the Associations' most famous members, Dr. Vojtech Alexander. He was born in Kežmarok on the 30th May, 1857, and was a pioneer of radiology in the Kingdom of Hungary. He brought the first X-ray apparatus to the area that is now Slovakia, from the US, and was the first doctor in the country to take an X-ray of a patient.

There were a few of the X-rays that Alexander had taken on display, some of human organs and also earlier ones of non-human X-rays, such as shells, eggs and a snake. One disturbing picture was of an X-ray of an unborn baby. Our guide told us how this X-ray was performed on a pregnant woman, at a time when Alexander was not fully aware of the dangers of radiation. The amount of radiation used was too much, and as a result the baby was born deformed. On that somber note, we left the room and headed for the final exhibition.

The last exposition was located on the ground floor and consisted of different items of equipment used by climbers in their conquest of the nearby Tatra Mountains. There was also a large painting that covered one of the walls in the room of all the mountains in the High Tatras. The painting showed the climber that was the first to conquer the peak, climbing that particular mountain. It was a great way of learning whom first triumphed over each of the different mountains, and when they achieved the feat.

Our guide told us that perhaps the most famous of all the visitors to the Tatras, and one of the first to venture into the smallest, high mountain range in the world, was a woman. She was in fact Beata Laska, the wife of one of the owners of Kežmarok Castle, who journeyed into her beloved Tatra Mountains without the permission of her husband. He was 17 years her junior, and had only married her for her money so that he could pay off his mounting gambling debts. For disobeying him, he had her imprisoned in the castle's tower for six years; ironically he made sure that his wife had a perfect view of the mountains. When she was finally let out of her prison, she had gone completely mad and died shortly afterwards.

By the time the tour of the castle had finished we were both feeling a little hungry, so we went to a small hotel on the main square for a spot of lunch. After a light meal, we made our way to the town art gallery, which was actually located in the same building as the tourist center. We found that the gallery was closed for refurbishment, so as it turned out we would have plenty of time to go back and look around the little, wooden church after all.

The protestant wooden articular church in Kežmarok was built in 1717, and the building is made entirely of wood, even the nails that hold it together. The style closely resembles the church, Norden Kerk, in Amsterdam, which was used as a prototype for many churches in Europe, at that time. The church was supposedly built by Swedish sailors, which may explain the round windows that look like the portholes of a ship.

The church was now open, so we went inside and were quite surprised at what we saw. Expecting to see a simple, drab interior, in keeping with the outside of the church, we were shocked to find that the inside was in fact quite bright, with richly colored walls.

"Wow, look at all the different paintings on the walls!" my wife exclaimed. "They are beautiful."

"Look at the ceiling then," I said.

Looking up, my wife saw how the ceiling had been painted to look like the sky. A bright blue sky, with thick white clouds, much the same as the one we had just left outside.

We then approached the altar, which was painted in rich colors of blue and green and ornately decorated with gold leaf. It included carved figurines of the crucifixion and various saints. I was itching to take a photo of this work of art, but had just spied one of the many placards on display, showing that cameras were not allowed to be used inside the church.

At the front of the church, an old lady, dressed in traditional village dress, dutifully collected donations for the church's upkeep. She also sold postcards and photos, some of which were professionally taken and really captured well the image before me. Having chosen a couple of the photos, I approached the woman to pay for them. As I took out the correct amount of money for my purchase, she gave me a toothless grin.

"Meričan?" she suddenly demanded, as I handed over 20Sk.

"Nie, Angličan!" I replied, wondering how these people could tell I was foreign before I'd even opened my mouth.

She then offered me a set of mini-postcards, which included pictures of the altar, font and pulpit, together with a written description of them, in English. I paid for these too, and wondered if she was working on commission. I then went and sat down next to my wife, who was seated at one of the pews, and read.

The informative postcards told me that a local wood carver, Jan Lerch, made the altar and pulpit between the years 1717 and 1727. It was hard to believe they were actually constructed from wood, as the artist had made such a fine job of making them look like marble. Immediately in front of the altar was a baptismal font, which was made of plain sandstone, but with a colorfully decorated lid. Apparently, the font pre-dated the church, having been made 27 years earlier in 1690.

Perhaps the most spectacular item of all though, was the church organ, which took up the entire back wall. The huge silver pipes, which rose up to the painted sky above, were also decorated with gold leaf, and at the very top of the organ there was a gold star. I read that this was a Baroque double keyboard organ and that it was in fact the oldest of its kind in Slovakia. Again, it was a surprise to see it here, inside what had initially appeared to be a simple parish church. After a while we left the wooden articulate church, wondering if the New Evangelical church, next door, would have been as impressive.

* * *

We were soon on our way to Levoča, relieved that nothing untoward had happened to the car whilst parked in Kežmarok. The journey lasted little more than half an hour, passing through Spišská Sobota and Poprad on the way. As we approached Levoča, we immediately saw signs for the hotel that

Ria had booked that morning. Five minutes later we had turned off the road and driven into the hotel car park.

"I don't like the look of that much," I said to my wife, as I looked at the miserable, gray building that we were supposed to spend the night in.

"Yes, and it's quite far from the town center as well," my wife agreed.

"Come on, let's see if we can find something better on the town square," I reasoned. "We can always come back here if there is nothing else available."

"Then lets hope that there is something else!" said my wife, looking again at the less than attractive hotel.

Searching for a new hotel turned out to be an excellent decision, because half an hour later we found ourselves in a luxurious suite, overlooking the town square, and all for a few hundred koruna more than the decidedly average hotel we had left, on the outskirts of town.

We had entered the main square through the Košická brána, one of the three remaining gates in the well-preserved town wall, which still surrounds Levoča. As soon as I saw the marvelous Master Pavol's square, with its numerous cultural and historical buildings, I fell in love with this beautiful city. The sixty or so colorful burgher houses that line the square, the green, well-kept parks, St. James' Cathedral, the Domed Evangelical Church, the interesting museums, and the many first class hotels, restaurants and bars, add up to make Levoča my favorite Slovak town. Pride of place, in the center of the square, is the most photogenic building in Slovakia, if not Central Europe, the wonderful Levoča Town Hall.

Of the three fine hotels on the square, we had chosen the mid-priced Arkadia, and had been extremely pleased with our choice. Now we relaxed in the suite-sized room that we had acquired for about $20, before getting showered and changed for the evening.

It was getting dark as we left the Arkadia for an early evening stroll. We took our time walking around the square, admiring the various buildings and deciding where we would visit the next day. Now and again, we popped into a bar and had a single beer, before moving on and continuing our walk. Eventually, we decided that we would eat, and chose the restaurant at another of the three hotels on the square, the even more plush, Hotel Satel.

As we entered the fine lobby of the Satel, we saw photos of distinguished guests that the hotel had played host to in the past; presidents and prime ministers, actors and novelists. We had found the best place in town, and the elegant atrium that we had just entered, confirmed this.

"Guess where we'll be having lunch tomorrow!" I exclaimed, as we looked at the café-style tables and chairs within the stylish courtyard.

"Yes, it's too cold to eat there tonight I suppose," said my wife. "Let's hope the restaurant is as nice."

The restaurant was superb, great food, great service, and at the right price too. Our waiter, on hearing us speaking English, began to tell us how he was currently learning English as well. He asked us how we liked Levoča, and told us the different places we should try and make the time to visit tomorrow. My wife spoke to him in Slovak, with me chipping in where I could. At the end of the meal, as he began to clear our plates away he turned to my wife and, thinking that he was paying her a big compliment, said:

"Where did you learn to speak such beautiful Slovak?"

"In Slovakia," my wife replied, a little taken aback. "I am Slovak!"

Bang goes your tip, I thought, and grinned as I saw the waiter's face turn a bright red.

"I'm so sorry," he began. "I thought you were English."

"No, I am Slovak, but I have been living in England for the last five years."

It was four and a half years actually, but she was obviously a little embarrassed that her accent had been mistaken as that of a foreigner's.

"Let's go and walk off our dinner," I said, after we had paid for the meal, together with a big tip I hasten to add.

The sky was now pitch black as we begun our walk, but it was a clear evening and the stars were sparkling. We strolled once more through the park, and after about half hour or so we made our way back to the hotel.

Not far from the hotel we spied a big cage, which our waiter had mentioned earlier. This was the fabled "Cage of Shame", built in the 16th Century, and used to punish perpetrators of minor crimes. They would be locked in there for a few days and humiliated.

"Okay, get behind the cage and make like your inside," I said to my wife, getting out my camera to take a picture.

"Why, what is my crime?" she joked.

"Forgetting how to speak Slovak!" I teased, and then deftly avoided a blow, before running back to the safety of the hotel.

Vol'by 2002 - Slovak General Election

Friday, early evening, on the 20th September 2002, and all across the country the people of Slovakia were arriving at polling stations to vote for their next government. Voters casting their votes before 14:00 on the Saturday, did so with the knowledge that this particular election would have a huge impact on their country's future.

The Slovak General Election (Vol'by) is slightly more complicated than elections back home. The Slovak voter doesn't just have to decide whether to vote for a left-wing, center, or right-wing party, instead they must choose between an incredible 25 political parties. With so many different parties, splitting so many of the votes, an outsider may be forgiven for thinking that it's all a bit of a lottery.

Vol'by 2002 is of particular importance to Slovakia. Membership to NATO and the European Union is not that far off for this small central European country, with a population of less than 6 million. However, it has been made crystal clear to Slovakia that she will not be allowed to join either organization if former Prime Minister, Vladimír Mečiar, is to play any part whatsoever in the new government.

It was Mečiar's HZDS party that led the various opinion polls leading up to the elections, extremely popular with pensioners throughout the country. In second place, not far behind HZDS was the young, populist lawyer, Robert Fico, and his SMER (direction) party. SMER had carried out an extensive election campaign, and the opinion polls showed that the youthful Fico was extremely popular amongst the country's first time voters. However, if the opinion polls were to be believed, neither of these left wing parties would secure the 51% of votes needed to form a government. It looked odds on that Slovakia would have another coalition government ruling the country, and as it was unlikely that any party would side with the Mečiar-led HZDS, Fico was perhaps the favorite to be Slovakia's next Prime Minister.

The current Prime Minister was Mikuláš Dzurinda, the leader of the SDK government, a coalition of a number of parties from throughout the political spectrum. Responsible for lifting Slovakia from the position of the black sheep of Central Europe, to a country on the brink of EU membership, Dzurinda is very well respected in the West. However, the tough economic measures that were needed to transform Slovakia have come at a price, and at home Dzurinda is largely seen as the man who has brought mass unemployment and rising prices to the country. Indeed, leading up to the election the opinion polls showed Dzurinda's new party, the SDKÚ, lying in third place, and a long way behind HZDS and SMER.

But then opinion polls rarely get these things spot on, and so on Friday afternoon, as my wife and her family went to a nearby school to cast their votes, I had a feeling that Voľby 2002 was going to be a close run thing.

* * *

My wife's old primary school had been transformed into a polling station for two days, and that is where we found ourselves at 7 o'clock, Friday evening. Outside a room containing two voting booths and a number of officials, a placard was hanging up listing the candidates for each of the 25 parties, side-by-side with a display of young children's paintings.

As well as choosing a party, the Slovak voters also had to decide on their preferred four candidates to represent them. While Ria and her parents went and voted, I stayed outside and studied the other 22 runners and riders, some of whom may well have a part to play in a coalition government. As well as HZDS, SMER and SDKÚ, the other main parties in the running were the right of center, ANO, the Christian Democratic party, KDH, and the party representing the large Hungarian minority in Slovakia, the SMK. Other parties that caught the eye were the Communist Party (KSS), the Nationalist Party (SNS), and the delightfully named "Women and Family" party*.

After Ria and her family had voted, we went on to the nearest pub, and like many others around us, we discussed how we thought the elections would pan out and who would be the best man to lead Slovakia over the next four years.

Saturday night, with the voting completed, we sat and watched an Election Special on Markiza, where the leaders of each of the top seven parties debated how the election was going and all the possible outcomes. The exit polls showed that HZDS were likely to win the most votes as expected, but the real surprises were firstly, how well the four right wing parties, SDKU, SMK, KDH and ANO were doing, and secondly, how badly SMER were doing. The biggest surprise of all though was the fact that the Communist Party, KSS, looked like they would secure an incredible 6% of the votes and come in seventh place.

*　*　*

By 10 o'clock, Sunday morning, the official results were in. The top seven of the 25 parties were as follows:

1. HZDS - 19.50% of votes cast - 560,691 votes - 36 seats
2. SDKÚ - 15.09% of votes cast - 433,953 votes - 28 seats
3. SMER - 13.46% of votes cast - 387,100 votes - 25 seats
4. SMK - 11.16% of votes cast - 321,000 votes - 20 seats
5. KDH - 8.25% of votes cast - 237,202 votes - 15 seats
6. ANO - 8.01% of votes cast - 230,309 votes - 15 seats
7. KSS - 6.32% of votes cast - 181,872 votes - 11 seats

President Schuster had given the leading parties 30 days to put forward a proposal for a new coalition government. It was highly unlikely that either Mečiar's HZDS or Fico's SMER would be able to get the support they needed to form a coalition government.

Meanwhile, it had been reported that Mikuláš Dzurinda had already put forward a proposal for a coalition between SDKÚ, SMK, KDH and ANO (together they had 78 seats, three more than the seventy five required), with himself as Prime Minister. It was thought that President Schuster was likely to accept this proposal within the next week.

And so it proved. Slovakia had a right of center coalition government for the next four years, a result that Europe and the

US had been hoping for and Slovakia's chances of gaining NATO and EU membership had increased dramatically.

* *(In case you were wondering the "Women and Family" party managed to get 12,646 votes, which was 0.43% of all votes cast).*

Sour Cabbage, Not Sour Grapes

Vlado had invited me to report on the making of Kapusta, the sour cabbage that is present in many of his recipes, most notably Kapustnica, my favorite Slovak soup. I had been extremely busy recently and Vlado had kindly put off making the Kapusta until I had a free evening. We had agreed on a Saturday night in October, Vlado saying that it really couldn't be put off any more. It wasn't until a couple of days before the Saturday it suddenly dawned on me that it would be the same day Slovakia would be playing England in their European Championships qualifier. And that was a match I didn't want to miss.

I arrived at Vlado's house at about half an hour before kick off, and was led through to the living room, where about a dozen friends and family members were sat in front of a television waiting impatiently for kick off. I said hello, and was greeted with some cheers and laughter when they saw the blue England cap I was wearing and the red, white and blue t-shirt that had ENGLAND written on it in big, bold letters. However, I hadn't the temerity quite yet to get the two Union Jacks out of my bag and start waving them around.

As I was led through to the kitchen, I saw a big, white vat, in the corner of the living room. Next to the vat was a bucket full of water, a towel and a chair. I noticed that the chair had a grandstand view of the television. Vlado saw me staring at the vat and grinned, then beckoned me into the kitchen. Once in the kitchen, Vlado showed me to a table, where he had neatly set out all the ingredients for making kapusta. There was beetroot, apples, horseradish, onions, garlic, salt, peppercorns and, of course, cabbages - a lot of cabbages.

Vlado handed me a bottle of beer and then suddenly asked me how much I weigh. I made the conversion from pounds to kilograms, and came out with about 80kg. Fine, he said, in that case I have got a job for you. I reached into my bag for my digital camera, as if to show him that I already had a job, and dutifully took a picture of the ingredients for the Slovakia -

Heart of Europe web site. Vlado viewed the picture, and then asked me how to operate the camera, as he said that I probably wouldn't be able to take any more pictures tonight. I was intrigued.

Vlado began making the Kapusta at about the same time as the match kicked off. I sat in the chair next to the vat, which gave me both a good view of the television and also of the kitchen, where Vlado and his daughter had begun to slice up the hundred or so cabbages. They used what looked like a giant cheese grater, and pushed each cabbage back and forth over the blade, so that the sliced cabbage fell into a huge, blue tub below.

Once I had got the general gist of how they were cutting up the cabbages, I helped myself to another beer and settled down to watch the game. I could tell by the jovial mood of everyone around me that Slovakia must be doing extremely well. England who were clear favorites to win the match, despite being away from home, had had a poor start to say the least. In fact, England were so bad in the opening twenty minutes or so, that I turned my attention back to what was happening in the kitchen.

While he and his daughter continued cutting up the cabbages, Vlado's wife began to add the sliced cabbage to the vat, the inside of which she had just smeared with an onion. Having added a layer of cabbage, she then added the horseradish, some of the beetroot and the apple quarters, a portion of the sliced onions and garlic, and a sprinkling of the salt and peppercorns. Once she had finished adding these ingredients, Vlado came over to inspect her work. Then he turned to me and told me that it was time that I began my job for the evening.

It was then that I found out that my 80kg would be put to good use, for I had somehow been volunteered to press the kapusta. This would involve me standing inside the vat and then stamping up and down on the layer of cabbage, apples, beetroot etc., until it had been pressed enough for the next layer to be added. I could hardly refuse, as Vlado had gone to all the trouble of placing the vat so that I had a good view of the football, which Slovakia were continuing to dominate.

Before I began treading the cabbage, I slipped off my shoes and socks and soaked my feet in the bucket of hot water. After a few minutes, I took my feet out of the bucket and dried them on the towel provided. As I was drying my feet, the unthinkable happened, Slovakia scored a goal. A huge cheer filled the room, then all eyes turned to me. There I was, with foot in hand, as a dozen Slovaks taunted me with cheers of "Jeden - nula" and "Slovensko, Slovensko !!!". I conceded that Slovakia well deserved their lead, and took another beer that was now offered, to help console myself.

With the first half drawing to a close, and England not showing any signs of improving, my attention turned back to the kapusta, and in particular the big white vat that I was just about to step into. I tentatively placed my right foot inside the vat, and felt my foot slowly sink into the cold cabbage, apples and beetroot mixture. Then I swung my left leg over the top of the vat, so that I stood on top of the kapusta, slowly sinking to about half way through the cabbage.

As it was now half time, the focus of attention turned from the television to the Englishman marching up and down on the cabbage in the corner of the room. I had been instructed by Vlado to imagine I was marching in a circle, and to apply particular pressure to the cabbage at the sides of the vat with my heels. I did as I was told, and after a short while I felt a cool liquid filling the bottom of the vat, as the juices were slowly squeezed from the various vegetables and fruit. After a while, the cabbage had been pressed down as far as it would go and the liquid had now risen to above my ankles.

I was told to get out of the vat, and placed my feet back into the bucket of water. Meanwhile, Vlado took a cup and started to bail out the liquid from the vat. The liquid was a light purple color, and after Vlado had drained a few cupfuls, he paused to have a sip. He then offered me the cup to taste, but I declined raising my bottle to show that I still had my beer. He proceeded to take another sip of the purple liquid and decided that a little more salt was necessary.

While Vlado and his wife began to add another layer of cabbage, apples and beetroot inside the vat, I joined in the discussion that was now taking place amongst the football fans, as to whether or not Slovakia would now be able to win the match. Some of the more pessimistic Slovaks argued that they were bound to lose as Slovakia had missed too many chances already, England were riding their luck and the referee was clearly England's 12th man. The younger, more optimistic Slovaks amongst us claimed that Slovakia would now go on to score three or four goals and give England a real thrashing. I sat firmly on the fence, and said I thought it might end up a draw.

By the time the second half was underway, I was back in the vat, marching up and down on the cabbage. By now, I had developed my technique somewhat, so that it wasn't long before the purple liquid was high above my ankles again and Vlado was draining it with the cup once more. As I sat with my feet in the bucket of water, while yet another layer of cabbage was added inside the vat, I saw that England were now beginning to play better and were having an equal share of the play. This coincided with a few of the decisions blatantly going England's way, which resulted in me learning a number of new Slovak expressions for how to describe a referee.

During my third stint in the vat, Vlado informed me that it was customary to toast the kapusta at this point. He then proceeded to open a nice Chardonnay and pour out a couple of glasses. So I stopped my marching for a moment, my feet half sunk in sodden cabbage, clinked glasses, said "Na zdravie", and began to enjoy a rather fine, white wine. It was exactly at this time that England scored an equalizer.

A fourth, fifth and sixth layer of cabbage was added to the vat in turn, which I dutifully stamped on, while all the time keeping my eyes fixed on the football match, which had at last become an interesting game. It was now end-to-end stuff, with both sides playing well, and having a fair number of chances. Then, nine minutes from the end, England scored what would prove to be the winner. Groans filled the room, followed by some more expletives aimed at the referee. As the final whistle blew, there was a somber mood, as the Slovaks present realized they would probably fail to qualify after this, their second defeat in a row. Meanwhile, I took little pleasure in England beating a team who had outplayed us for most of the game. The Union Jacks remained in my bag.

After the sixth and final layer of cabbage had been pressed, Vlado placed a heavy stone on a plate and put it on top of the kapusta, and we then carried the vat to a corner of the kitchen, where it would stay for the next six weeks to ferment. I looked around the room at everyone, who were still ruing the missed chances, and blaming the referee. At least the evening hadn't been a total disappointment I thought to myself. After all, they had kapustnica to look forward to, courtesy of an Englishman.

Christmas Shopping

With less than four weeks to go until Christmas, my wife and I have managed a first, not only have we sent all the Christmas cards to both sets of relations and friends, we have also finished all of our Christmas shopping. No last minute panicking as to what to buy Uncle Ján this year, or whether cousin Katka needs a new scarf and glove set. No, the presents have been bought and wrapped, and we can now sit back and relax, and enjoy the run up to Christmas.

So what is the reason for this amazing efficiency? What have we done differently this year, to any other year? What is the secret to our success? Well, simply put, last week we went to Tesco.

Now, let me tell you that the Tesco stores in Slovakia are a little different to those back home. These aren't big Supermarkets that sell groceries, a few lines of clothes, some CDs, books and magazines, etc. No, the Slovak Tesco hypermarkets are simply gigantic, and they sell EVERYTHING! It is not unheard of for my wife to spend a whole weekend wandering up and down the myriad of aisles in a Slovak Tesco. And last Thursday I actually joined her for almost a whole afternoon, on the proviso that we bought everybody's Christmas present in one fell swoop.

Now, as it turned out we weren't only shopping for Christmas presents. Ria's family is so big that we were also shopping for about three people's birthdays and five different namesdays, which happened to fall in and around the Christmas period. Added to that, we also had to buy a selection of goodies for each of our many nephews, nieces and godchildren, to fill their boots on St. Nicholas Day, on the 6th December.

St. Nicholas Day is celebrated throughout Slovakia, where kids up and down the country take one of their boots and clean it on the evening of the 5th, and then leave it out overnight for St. Nicholas to fill with small toys, chocolates and sweets. It's a lovely tradition, but I can't help remembering that two of my little nieces have recently been bought knee length, red boots, that will no doubt hold more chocolate and sweets than you could reasonably eat from now until Christmas. I am sure this is just a coincidence, but you can bet your bottom dollar which boots they'll be cleaning on the 5th.

After a couple of hours or so, with most of the big presents having been chosen, I decided that I had had enough of advising my wife on whether the snowman serviettes would be more suitable than the Rudolph ones, and went off for a little wander. In actual fact, I went Brand Spotting. From a young age, whenever I was on holiday in Europe, I always enjoyed wandering around supermarkets, trying to find those foreign brand names that just wouldn't sell back home. Every English schoolboy, on a day trip to France, is sure to purchase a bottle of Sic at some point, which is in fact a fizzy orange drink that sometimes lives up to its name on the ferry back home to Dover.

So far, Slovakia has given us Hell beer (which is actually exported to the UK), Fanny toilet paper, and the delightful Snoty sugar. However, I was determined to find more and funnier brand names, and so while my wife was working out how many of the different types of wrapping paper we would need, I began my quest. Half an hour later and I was beginning to get bored. I had already exhausted frozen foods, canned goods, toiletries, and even the pet food section, and had found nothing really worth a mention. I decided that I would just give the drink aisle a quick try, and then go off in search of my wife.

Then suddenly I saw it. The ultimate funny brand name. There it was in a choice of apple and blackberry flavor or fruit of the forest. I looked at it again. Surely in my eagerness to find a funny brand name I had misread the label. But no, I had not misread the label at all. I had in fact discovered Fart.

Such was the design of the label, the word Fart had actually been written many times on the bottle, in different fonts and colors. They have even registered it! Yes, its true, Fart is a registered brand name in Slovakia. A thought suddenly crossed my mind. What if this was exported back home, think of the money to be made. It would be every schoolboy's dream, to take out a bottle of Fart from his lunch box, and show it to his friends. Fart would no doubt soon outsell Pepsi Cola and Coca-Cola and become the number one selling soft drink. With these entrepreneurial thoughts spinning around my head, I picked up a crate of Fart and went off to find my wife.

I found Ria at the nut counter, weighing a large bag of cashew nuts. I eagerly began to present to her my recent discovery, when the shop's speaker system began relaying an announcement, and I was unceremoniously told to shush!

"What was that about?" I asked, wondering what on earth could be more important than Fart.

"I couldn't hear it properly, because of your messing about!" replied my wife. "But I think she said that if you spend more than 600Sk today you get a free chicken and a kilogram of rice."

"Excellent!" I said, always happy to get a freebie. "If we have got everything, let's go and pay for it all now, in case they run out of chickens."

By the time we got to the checkout, I had worked out that 600Sk was only about US $15, and I had come up with an ingenious plan.

"Okay, you take a few things and pay for them in cash, and then I'll follow behind and pay for the rest on my credit card," I reasoned to my wife. "That way we'll get two chickens."

Reluctantly, she agreed, and went ahead of me and paid for about 2000Sk worth of stuff. I then followed, with the rest of our shopping, which by now was almost spilling from the trolley, and settled the bill with my credit card.

"We have to take our receipts over there!" said Ria, pointing to a counter on the far side of the store, by the exit. "And they'll give us the chicken and the rice."

"Okay, you go first!" I said. "And make it look like we're not together, in case they have some rule about only one chicken per household."

So Ria went off in front, and I followed at a short distance, determined to get two free chickens, my Scottish half coming to the fore. How my wee mammie would be proud of me, I thought to myself. My wife handed over her receipt, and to our surprise, she was given three chickens and 3Kg of rice. It wasn't until I too had handed over my receipt that it suddenly dawned on me that 2000Sk was roughly three times 600Sk, hence the three chickens and the 3Kg of rice. Obviously Ria had also just done the math, as she looked at me alarmingly and slowly her face began to have a little pink glow.

Sure enough, the man behind the counter, having checked the receipt a number of times, proceeded to call out to his assistant "23" in a rather loud voice. "23?" came the astonished assistants reply, also rather too loud for my liking, and once he was satisfied that his colleague wasn't joking, he proceeded to load 23 chickens and 23Kg of rice on to a nearby trolley. I was suddenly aware that there was now a crowd of people queuing up for their chicken and that all eyes were on us. Ria, who was now almost a burgundy color, put her three chickens and rice in my trolley, as well as another couple of bags of shopping, while at the same time giving me one of those looks that says "this is all your fault".

Then, without saying a word and with all the composure in the world, she skillfully maneuvered her trolley-full of Christmas shopping through the crowd and led the way to our car. I followed, my head held high, pushing the other trolley, which now carried our 26 chickens, 26Kg of rice, and ten bottles of Fart.